T0129407

LeadershipTips

LeadershipTips

Common Sense Thoughts for Uncommon Times

Carter Campbell

iUniverse, Inc.
New York   Bloomington

LeadershipTips
Common Sense Thoughts for Uncommon Times

The views expressed in this work are solely those of the author and do not
necessarily reflect the views of the publisher, and the publisher hereby
disclaims any responsibility for them.

iUniverse books may be ordered through booksellers or by contacting:

iUniverse
1663 Liberty Drive
Bloomington, IN 47403
www.iuniverse.com
1-800-Authors (1-800-288-4677)

Because of the dynamic nature of the Internet, any Web addresses or links
contained in this book may have changed since publication and may no
longer be valid.

ISBN: 978-1-4502-0333-3 (sc)
ISBN: 978-1-4502-0334-0 (ebk)

Printed in the United States of America

iUniverse rev. date: 01/06/2010

Dedication

To Roi, my wonderful wife, best friend and life coach who makes it all happen through her unconditional love, encouragement and wisdom.

Contents

Forward

This little book began about five years ago. I am a Registered Nurse, and at that time I was working as a training and organizational development specialist. Our organization had fallen on hard times and was about to be sold to a much larger company. One of my colleagues made a comment about the rapid amount of change we were experiencing. I must say I had to agree.

I have been a student of organizational, team and personal dynamics for many years, so within these pages you will see the influence of some of the greatest minds in this field: Drucker, Maxwell, Collins and Covey. However, the first seed of this book didn't come from any of theirs. You see, layoffs, new leadership, and rumors of closings left a lot of unsettled feelings in our organization, and as an effort to ease some of my colleagues' concerns, I wrote my first leadership tip on change that day. I sent it out by e-mail and, unlike most inter-office memos; I received a lot of positive feedback. Encouraged, I began writing short and to the point useful tips to both my clients and colleagues to address what I and others were going through—normal organizational issues addressed from a constructive yet realistic perspective.

Communicating during changing times

There are hundreds, no, thousands of books, tapes and materials that teach about communication. Colleges offer degrees in communication. But good communication doesn't require a degree. With a healthy dose of common sense, it's easy to get it right when you are dealing with personal, team and organizational communication.

Most organizations go through more than their fair share of change and will continue to go through change. One of the keys to successfully navigating change is to communicate effectively at all levels of the organization—top down and bottom up. Here are a few tips for "getting it right" when dealing with your next communication challenge

Make your communication two-way.

You have two ears and one mouth for a reason. We often miss important information and cultural dynamics in our team meetings if all we do is read off a list of bullet points. Take time to ask your team to comment on a situation or provide feedback.

Be aware of how you feel about the situation.

We communicate with more than the words we use. Our tone of voice, body language and mannerisms can convey our feelings regarding a situation without our even knowing it. Whether you are in a delicate conversation with an employee, or loved one, or if you are communicating a message that may be hard, be careful, not only of your word choices but your body language as well. I will address this in more detail in the "What's Your Message?"chapter of this book.

Be sure the message is ready for publication.

In any leadership position, one often has the opportunity to hear opposing viewpoints and ideas for the future in the safety of a closed environment. Not every discussion at a leadership level is what I call "mature" enough to go out for public discussion. If your work, team, meeting or discussion sentences begin with, *"We think," "It may be,"* or *"We believe,"* you should probably think VERY carefully about how you are going to communicate the message. As a leader, if you are not sure of what you are saying, how can your team members trust what you are saying?

Say what you mean, mean what you say, but don't say it mean.

Have the courage to say what needs to be said and the consideration to say it in a manner that keeps egos and interests intact. In other words, say what you mean, mean what you say, but don't say it mean. I've worked with many work teams where someone has been labeled as "a complainer." Usually, if I spend time with that person, the issue is that they have the courage to say what needs to be said. They just lack the consideration to say it in a way that people will listen, Because of this, their message—often an important one—gets lost. If you're one of these people, see the first section.

In closing, I'm not suggesting you keep information from team members. Quite the contrary. I believe in flooding team members with as much knowledge as we can give them, as long as it is accurate and clear. The more people understand their company's direction; the better off the company is in executing its strategic goals.

Our communication techniques have a huge influence on our team's morale and how well we navigate change. Ram Charan said it best:

> *"To deal with change you must manage your social system, and information flow in the social system is the oxygen... dialogue."*

Application

Is your communication two-way?

How do you feel about the situation?

Is your message ready for publication?

During your last emotional interaction, were you destructive or constructive?

What steps will you take at your next team meeting to be a more effective communicator?

_____

_____

_____

_____

Managing 360 Degrees

What do you think of when you hear the term "managing up?" To Quint Studer, Health Care Customer Service guru, managing up means proactively feeding your leaders information regarding your department and the people that work in it, so that the leader can address you and your team's needs on a more personal level. Roseanne Badowski, Assistant to Former GE CEO Jack Welch, authored the book Managing Up: How to Form an Effective Relationship with Those Above You –an excellent source on how to take care of your boss. There is absolutely nothing wrong with either of these techniques, and I believe they should be practiced. But I also believe that we need to broaden our sphere of thinking and go beyond "managing up" to managing 360 degrees. Not only should we understand the strengths and weaknesses of those who work above us, we should also understand the strengths and weaknesses of those who work beside us, and those whom we supervise. By understanding the strengths and weaknesses of our "team," and I mean that inclusively of anyone who works with you, we are better able to help them, and they are able to help us.

When we manage 360 we build trust and encourage reciprocation. The simple act of being aware of those who we need to help and those who can help you builds teamwork. Managing 360 also means protecting people even when they don't know they need protection. If you know someone will be hurt by a relational transaction you make sure they are protected. The trust that is built will help you move quicker and faster in the future when people know you care for them.

Another application to "managing 360 degrees" is being sure that credit is given where credit is due. Be sure that when you have the opportunity to celebrate the contribution of others, you seize the moment and make sure, with great intention, that you name them.

I watched once as a senior leader passed a team member in the hallway and complimented her with specificity on a job well done. The team member knew that her manager had made a report of the project earlier in the day. She also knew that the manager didn't have any reason to mention her name. She now knows that the manager was conscientious enough to mention her contribution, even when she wasn't in the room. This powerful trust-building action for this team member and manager didn't cost a dime but had a huge return on investment. Managing 360 isn't a task thing, it's an accountability and character thing, and it has huge returns for your moral authority.

One man cannot hold another man down in the ditch without remaining down in the ditch with him. Booker T. Washington

Application

Do you know the strengths and weaknesses of your team members?

Do you protect the interests of others as well as your own?

Do you give credit where credit is due, intentionally?

What relationship dynamic do you need to address to become a more effective leader?

_____

_____

_____

_____

_____

_____

_____

_____

Team Building

Team building, the term automatically conjures up ropes courses, people falling backward into the arms of their colleagues, blindfolds and the like. These techniques don't actually create teamwork; they point out the importance of trust in teams. Techniques practiced in seminar-land are useless unless the participants begin to act on the lessons learned. But, as with many programs, managers are looking for a quick fix day to correct the greater underlying monster of mistrust that is driven by the behaviors that remain in the workplace.

"Making promises generates hope, keeping promises generates trust." - Blaine Lee

Trust is the foundation of building any team. Trust is built in many ways, but at its most basic, it simply means keeping the promises we make to each other. It means you will follow through on items that support the work your team members are trying to get done. Use honest straightforward communication. Very rarely when I work with groups on trust and teamwork is the leader's character questioned. When it is, and I dig deeper, the issue usually is described by statements that start like this: *"She never..." "I asked and he didn't..."* You get the picture. Lack of follow through. Leaders can't meet every need. And if you can't, you need to approach your team with honesty, saying "*I can't do that because...*" This is one time when bad news is better than no news.

Sometimes you have to kick someone off the team.

Team mistrust isn't always the fault of the team leader. Team members with hidden agendas or misguided expectations can also be a factor. People get cranky at work for more reasons than we can consider in this brief tip. Suffice it to say, it happens and should be confronted in a coaching manner. Sometimes people don't even realize that their behavior has become disruptive. It can sometimes be a symptom of an unmet need, but if you grease a squeaky wheel and it continues to be a problem, you have to replace it.

Some "watch outs" for team building

- Don't sacrifice the organization to make yourself look good in front of your crew. Remember that the "they" you are talking about is YOU if you are in management.

- Be careful that you are not focusing so much on a team member's individual needs that you don't get the work of your unit done.

- True teamwork comes from accountability. Some people mistake the absence of discipline as a means of building a team, when in fact it's the lack of accountability that destroys the team.

Team Building "Dos"

- Involve your team in decision making regarding unit activities. Solicit participation and celebrate contribution often.

- Follow through on the requests that you take on, even if it means simply reporting back "no" to a request.

- Be "loyal to the absent," a term from Stephen Covey's *7 Habits of Highly Effective People.* Don't talk about other team members who are not present with the team members who are. If you do, they'll wonder what you say about them when they aren't around.

- Pitch in. Never be too big or too busy to every once in awhile step into the day-to-day work of your unit and work with your team.

- Set people up for success. If you empower your staff or give someone a project, monitor the progress and be a barrier buster for things that may be getting in their way. Make sure they are set up to be successful and celebrate their achievement as a team.

- Praise in public, coach in private.

These are just a few tips for team building. As you can see, it's not about an exercise or a retreat. Those may be helpful in getting things started, but the real key to team building is your actions. They speak so much louder than your words.

Application

How is your follow through?
What will you do today to actively build trust?
Is there behavior on your team that you should confront?

List the action steps you will take this week to improve team-work.

_____

_____

_____

_____

What's Your Message?

What's your message? No, not what you say. Rather, what message do you convey with your actions and body language? What are you telling people around you by your actions and attitude? We can instill fear or confidence by simple acts of how we return from a meeting, communicate change, describe our jobs, and at the very core, how we carry ourselves.

Be aware of how you carry yourself.

I was visiting my mom while she was an inpatient for surgery in a hospital a few years ago. When the nurse came in she was in a hurry, flustered and moving quickly about the room. I had seen this nurse before and she seemed very capable on my first visit. I observed the fear and mistrust on my mom's face as she watched caregiver who said all the right things, and took all the right actions, and did it with the grace of a bull in a china shop. The "way" she went about caring spoke much louder than the care itself. Half-way through the morning, my mother, who is a very proper person, simply stated "get me outta here!"

My observation? Clinically this nurse performed well. Unfortunately that didn't translate to her actions. How often do we as leaders make the same mistake?

We need to be aware of our feelings and reactions to situations so that we can lead effectively and understand the messages that we send. How we act speaks so much louder than what we say.

Think about the impact you are having.

Think about your reactions and your message. How do you carry yourself? Our co-workers need to feel safe to discuss operational issues so that we can look for ways to make their jobs easier. How you handle the conversation—constructively or destructively—drives the emotional side of the discussion. Do you confess the sins of the organization and commiserate with your staff to make yourself look good or,do you provide rationale, confidence and answers to your team?

Many of the company transitions and changes we go through require some complex and difficult conversations. As leaders, we still have the lion's share of responsibility for our department's culture. I am not saying it's easy. We certainly need to be able to express issues and problems with our supervisors and each other in a constructive manner to look for resolutions. If we expect our staff to have an "on stage" demeanor with customers, so must we as leaders have "on stage" with them and "off stage" to discuss issues with our peers and our supervisors. The best messages are given with honesty, truth and explanation. If you don't have the answer, then sometimes we need to "manage up" and ask the right questions before we talk with our staff.

Leadership means taking responsibility. Responsibility means we are "response" "able." We can match our response to the situations. As leaders do you instill fear and insecurity, or confidence and direction?

Application:

How do you carry yourself, Confident or questionable?

What impact are you having on your staff, be honest

What will you do to control the way you present yourself to others?

_____

_____

_____

_____

Tips for Effective Meetings

Meetings, meetings and more meetings! Here are a few tips to make your next meeting more productive.

1. Have a goal - What do you want to accomplish in your meeting?

A fact we forget...MEETINGS COST MONEY...I was with a group of executives who were called together to make some pretty easy decisions. They were engaged in social conversation and not focused on the agenda when the CEO walked in and simply stated, "We're spending an awful lot of money in this room, let's get something done!" Next time you're in a meeting, try this exercise: add up all of the dollars you suspect are being spent on wage and salary for the people sitting in the room. You'd be amazed at how quickly it adds up. If you're in a meeting that's going nowhere you've got to ask yourself the question, "Is this the most productive use of my time?" and "How much are we costing the company right now?"

2. Elicit participation

If no one is talking in your meeting you can ask simple open-ended questions to elicit dialogue. *What do you think about that? What can your team contribute to this project?*

3. Look for hidden agendas

As long as there are motives and incentives there will be dissenting opinions. Be careful to consider the motives of the people on your team. Are they working from a "Me" or a "We" point of view? Are people talking about the potential issues of the project that can lead to failure so they can address them? Every project has critical "go/no go" decision points. Ask the hard questions, *"What can cause this to fail?" "What will keep us from our goal?"* A problem defined is often a problem half solved. If you're on the other side of the equation, use appropriate word choices and be tactful.

4. Assign responsibilities and agree on deadlines

Decide who is responsible and accountable for action steps that will carry your ideas forward from the meeting. This usually begins with having an identified outcome or "reason to meet" before you even start the meeting. (See tip one.)

5. Reward success

Celebrate the successes of the individuals and the team. For those who aren't achieving their goals, having an "offline" conversation will allow for better, more honest, communication and coaching. In addition it will help the under-achiever save face, and quite frankly, help you determine if you have the right person for the right job.

6. Have closure at the end of each meeting.

Save the last few minutes of your meeting to recap your accomplishments. Review your progress and be sure that everyone is clear on your next steps and timelines. Every action item should have a champion assigned and proposed deadline

Application:

Ask, what is your reason for the meeting?
Consider your destination; what decisions do you want to have by the end of the meeting?
Have you made assignments with deadlines?

_____

_____

_____

_____

_____

How to Create a Silo

I'm not speaking of a grain storage silo; I'm talking about the cold war missile silos that were built for the policy of mutually assured destruction. The organizational silo is one where you dig a deep hole in the organization—one where no one can find you or communicate with you. You are suspect of all messages coming in. You don't trust ANY communication from the outside unless you filter it through your own secret decoder ring. You don't have anything to do with any of the other silos in your organization, lest such communication interfere with your independent mission. From an organizational point of view, turf wars and silos assure mutual destruction of interdependent organizational goals. But some people don't know that they are in a silo. Consider these scenarios.

- Hal Lackaby has been known to ask other departments to extend themselves to benefit his staff, without thinking how his people might contribute to the project at hand.

- Donna Britton rarely attends leadership meetings, knowing that she'll be informed later of any really important decisions.,

- Last week, Yolanda Herrera stormed into another leader's department to defend the honor of one of her team members without knowing both sides of the story.

- William Carlson charged into another department to confront another team's employee without notifying that employee's supervisor of the conversation.

If you answered "yes" to any of these questions then take your finger off the "launch" switch, step back and consider the damage you are doing to your team. It's almost like taking a gun, putting it to your head proclaiming, "everyone back, I have a hostage!"

The only way out of a silo is to recognize when you're in one. Take the list above and do the opposite of what it tells you.

- Involve other departments in interdependent discussions, especially if they need to be part of the solution. Think about what your department might be contributing or could do to alleviate the problem.

- If you think you have the solution before the meeting, subordinate those thoughts until everyone has been heard, then offer up the solution. Chances are, by the time everyone is finished discussing the issues, your solutions will be modified to the best fit for all of the stakeholders in the situation.

- Attend informational meetings as well as work meetings. In many situations you are the only information conduit that your staff has to the outside world. Be sure you are bringing information back to your staff and if you have delegated a meeting to someone on your team, ask for a report.

- Keep leadership lines of communication open. Avoid "we/they" discussions that make you look good at the expense of another department or person. Seek all points of view before landing on a decision. Be sure that if it involves another department that you don't break the chain of command.

Leaders have an awful lot of responsibility when it comes to shaping corporate culture. Which do you want, a culture of cooperation or a culture of contempt?

You cannot live independently in an interdependent world—

Stephen R. Covey

Application:

Do I involve other departments or associates in interdependent problems?

Do I attend enough leadership meetings to know what is going on?

Have I communicated direction with my team?

_____

_____

_____

_____

_____

Common Sense Isn't Always Common Practice

I was thinking about how often we forget to take care of each other and ourselves, and how often common sense isn't common practice. We know that if we treat each other well, others will usually treat us well. Conversely, we know that if we act cranky, people will often give cranky in return, or just out-and-out avoid us. We've heard the phrase, "if momma ain't happy, ain't nobody happy." The same holds true for leaders at the Senior, Director and Team Leader levels. And let's not forget those informal leaders who have such a huge impact on the social culture of our departments.

Stephen Covey uses the metaphor of an Emotional Bank Account, which equates to the amount of trust that exists in a relationship. This concept works on an organizational, departmental and individual level. Deposits increase trust, withdrawals decrease trust. As with bank accounts, there is a return on investment, an ROI if you will. The more you smile, use the right language, keep the right attitude and tone, the more other people are willing to do the same. The more you frown and refuse to help unless helped first, the less people are willing to do things to help you.

We need to watch out for each other, both leader to leader and leader to team member. Look for warning signs that tell us someone needs a rest. Add these to your daily checklist:

- How many times have you played referee this week?

- Have you had to respond to customer service complaints so much that you have the service recovery department on speed dial?

- How many times this week have you heard "*that's not my job,*" or "*that's not my customer?*"

All of these are signs of staff in need of rest or redesigned systems and processes. We must keep a balance between our work and our rest. Equipment, people and machines have breaking points if they are not taken care of. We know that employee and customer incidents and accidents go up when people are fatigued. Sometimes we are so happy to have someone cover a shift or come in to take care of an issue that we overlook the fact that they just finished giving us 50 hours. The most effective coaches know when to pull a player and give him a rest so that he can finish the game. So too, the most effective leaders recognize the system flaws that create more work and when NOT to ask someone to pull the extra shift.

When was the last time that you thanked your staff for going the extra mile or thought twice before asking the person that you know would say *yes*, when they should say *no*, to pull extra duty?

Systems and processes are the engine of an organization, but people are the fuel.

—*Carter Campbell*

Application

Have you reviewed your systems and process lately to be sure you have the best productivity?

Has anyone on your team been working extra overtime?

Have you done any renewal activities with yourself or your team lately?

_____

_____

_____

_____

_____

And vs. But – getting to cooperation

As leaders, it is helpful to use facilitation skills. Facilitation defined is "to make easier." As facilitators we are called upon to look past the topsoil of communication and to dig down to the clay. Some of that digging means clearing verbal rocks out of the way that might keep us from reaching our objective. If you find yourself facilitating a group and the word "*but*" keeps coming up, then you've hit one of those rocks, and it will be primarily for one of two reasons:

To stop someone else's idea so that they can share their own or...

To let the other people on the team know there is a problem with the idea.

Both situations can become toxic to the facilitation process. The facilitated method is to get this language out of the group and get them to "*and*" through a gentle verbal nudge.

If the word "*but*" is being used to block an idea so that another one can be told, facilitators can look for the "*and*" in the situation. Listen to both sides and look for the common ground. For example:

MARK: I think we can use e-mail to communicate the newsletter.

MARJORIE: But not everyone has e-mail.

Marjorie's statement may be correct but it lacks a solution, stopping the creative process. A facilitator can bring the "and" out of them by asking, "What do you think is an appropriate solution?" An answer might be, "we can have town hall meetings." Take the answer they come up with and use "and" to link the two ideas together to create teamwork and inclusiveness. The example, "Could we use e-mail to communicate the information "*and*" have town hall meetings?"

In this tip we concentrated on how a facilitator might use the word "and" to get past opposing views. We can also use the same technique in many different interactions, both formal and informal. It's a simple linking word, but one that can go a long way to breaking down silos, valuing differences of opinion and creating teamwork. So, how many rocks have you moved or kicked over today?

None of us is as smart as all of us -- Ken Blanchard

Application

Consider your thoughts and speech during your next meeting.

Do you foster cooperation or is it my way or the highway?

Whose ideas need to be considered?

Are there two ideas that can be blended into one?

_____

_____

_____

_____

_____

It's about relationships

The month of February highlights relationships. We usually think about our romantic relationships, but it's a good time to reassess all of our relationships, both personally and professionally. Personally and professionally we often get caught up in the "tasks" at work and at home. But life, like business, thrives on the strength and amount of trust that exists with the people we live with and the people we work with. No matter how efficiently you execute a task or issue an executive decree to the troops, the chances of the task or decree being implemented and the quality of the execution hinges on the amount of trust you have established. Trust is built by taking care of people's needs, both emotionally and tangibly. In our personal relationships, it's important to understand what the significant people in our lives need from us and then meet those needs. Our professional lives, are much the same, but with the added responsibility of removing the barriers that keep our team members from doing what they want to do. Deliver. How do we figure that out? Through a little imagination, observation and execution which will work both at work and at home.

Imagination, Observation, Execution:

We all know what we want our relationships to look like, but we often spend more time planning our vacations than planning our relationships. Yes, I said it, planning our relationships: thinking about our relationships and how we want them to be and what we want them to look like. Once you have that vision in your head you can think about your current realities, the where you are now compared to where you want to be. But I have to take a time out for a hint. *If what you have in your head is what the other people in your life can do to make the relationship better, you've missed the boat.* Change starts with you. Go back to step one, Imagine what you want the relationships at work and home to be, then think about what YOU can do different to make it better.

The biggest opportunity we have to improve our relationships and our environment at work and at home is to think about where we want our relationships to be. We need to assess where we are, then get to work on the attributes that are missing to create the work and home environments that we want to live in. This time I leave you two quotes:

Let us be the change we seek in the world. Mahatmas Gandhi

And

The values you live by create the world you live in.

- Blaine Lee

Life is about relationships, not tasks.

Application

What will you do to make your relationships better, both personally and professionally? Once you have identified them, what's keeping you from execution?

_____

_____

_____

_____

_____

Forgive - to pardon an offense or an offender

I was listening to a sermon on forgiveness and started to think about how it relates to leadership. Forgiveness or lack thereof can have grave consequences for us as leaders. It certainly goes much deeper than just leadership; it goes to all aspects of our lives.

Personal Forgiveness

Forgiving ourselves for past mistakes can undo the paralytic fear of repeating the past, or worse, living our lives in it. Holding a grudge against yourself makes about as much sense as holding yourself hostage at gun point. It is one of the worst forms of self- punishment and so unnecessary. So, keep the lesson, throw away the torture. We must look hard at our failures, learn from them, and decide what we would do if we found ourselves in a similar situation in the future. Forgive yourself, take a step forward, and then move on.

Interpersonal Forgiveness

Interpersonal forgiveness from a leadership perspective is essential to our effectiveness and fairness as leaders. Through my facilitation practice I've found myself in conflict resolution situations where the parties involved simply can't let go of past failures, leaving both sides ineffective. Conflict situations are tough when they are peer to peer; they are devastating when it is leader to direct report. At the end of the day the only actions we truly can control, sometimes questionably, are our own—our reaction to the situations we are placed in. As leaders, a lack of forgiveness can cloud our judgment and jade our interactions with the person who is the target of our anger, hurt or pain. It's a trust-destroyer and huge detriment to team effectiveness and both parties lose. Many times the act of not forgiving hurts the offended worse than the offender. It's like drinking a cup of poison to get back at someone else.

Dealing with interpersonal forgiveness can be tricky. Sometimes the person you think you need to forgive doesn't even know they have wronged you.

- If the person in the interaction knows they have wronged you and asks for forgiveness, grant it and move on.

- If you are the one needing forgiveness, and the other party knows it, meet with that person and sincerely ask for their forgiveness.

- If you need to forgive someone who does not know they have offended you, or doesn't think that what they did was wrong, quietly forgive them inside without reliving the experience with them or reopening a wound.

In other words, the last scenario is done in your heart, not out loud. Many well-meaning people have approached someone they felt was an offending party only to find out the person didn't even know they had done anything that was perceived as wrong. "Getting something off your chest" is not always constructive. Judith Martin said "The one prediction that NEVER comes true is "*you'll thank me for telling you this.*"

Finally, a common misunderstanding of forgiveness is that it requires two parties, it doesn't. It just requires someone to have enough character and humility to realize we all make mistakes and a desire to live out of the future, not the past. We can't go back and change the past, but we can begin today to create a new future.

> *Forgiveness is letting go of a hope for a better past.*

> – Anonymous

Application

Who do you need to forgive?

What relationships are in need of repair professionally?

What relationships are in need of repair personally?

Are you willing to do what you need to do to repair them?

_____

_____

_____

_____

_____

Read Your Organization's Road Signs

Another set of goals. It's the first business day after the planning session. How are you doing? Day one should be pretty easy to accomplish, but how will you be doing six months from now? Will you have made the changes necessary to meet the needs of the organization and your people?

A coach watches the players, observes the competition and makes adjustments to strategy throughout the game. When a plane is placed on autopilot, the pilot still watches the navigation controls and makes course adjustments throughout the journey. We as leaders of our businesses and departments within larger organizations must do likewise.

Read the gauges, watch the players

Every organization has metrics they use to measure success. These measures can be formal or informal. It can be the CFO financial report, customer satisfaction scores or productivity. The key is to pay attention to them. Business and project outcomes, financial health, customer service scores and team member turnover can be a great starting place to help you make your own course corrections to achieve your goals. In addition, watching your players, what they do and how efficiently they do it, can help you in coaching your team to greater success. No game plan was ever instituted if the coach didn't communicate the goals and the game plan to the players.

Make course adjustments

I have worked with individuals and organizations that have done a great job of deciding where they want to go; they've gone so far as to create one- to five-year plans. The trouble is that when the gauges and compass tell them it's time to course correct or to trade a player, they don't make the tough call. They become so entrenched in the plan that they forget the purpose. If they were flying a plane and the destination lay on the other side of a mountain, they would ignore all the evidence and fly into the mountain instead of changing their flight plan. This concept of reading the gauges and paying attention works when examining your personal, interpersonal and organizational impact. We should expect change daily.

Personally

How is your health? Are you taking time to recharge yourself so that you can take care of others? This is the foundation which enables us to take care of interpersonal and organizational issues. If you haven't taken care of yourself you won't be able to take care of your interpersonal and organizational issues. Your focus will be off.

Interpersonally

Have you communicated your goals to the team? Do you regularly check with them to see how things are going or what can be done better? What processes need to change so that you can achieve your interdependent goals?

Organizationally

Do you and your supervisor/director/VP have mutually agreed-upon goals that support the organization? Have you agreed on what you both will consider success?

The whole affects the parts and the parts affect the whole.

One final thought as you lead forward to accomplish your goals. Most organizations are complex and require a tremendous amount of teamwork. You may be visionary in your solutions, but they still need to be gut-checked with the other departments and people that will be impacted or need to implement the solution. When you come up with an idea, your next step should be to consider who else will be impacted by that idea and how to involve them in the solution.

Application

What metrics will tell you the health of your organization?

What is the baseline of those metrics?

How often do you need to review them?

When will you know you are in trouble?

_____

_____

_____

_____

_____

Succession planning

Time for your vacation again but you just can't bring yourself to get away can you? You wanted to go to that off site meeting but you just can't leave your team alone. When you look around for someone to step into your shoes while you're gone you don't see anyone you think is capable. Guess what, that's your bad. A healthy organization builds its bench strength by mentoring future leaders.

One of the crucial roles of a leader is to mentor and bring up future leaders. We need to be able to cultivate and release the power and potential of those who are following us.

Two Paradigms of Succession planning

Let me give you two paradigms for you to think about. Do a little self-assessment to see which one fits you:

Paradigm A

"I have my team assembled, I like them just the way they are, and I want them to take care of the day to day operations. If they will just concentrate on the tasks of my work unit, I can concentrate on what my supervisor wants from me"

Paradigm B

"I have my team assembled, but two people on my team have expressed a desire to take on more responsibility. I am going to take extra time with each of them to mentor both management and leadership skills. I'll give them more responsibility and time to help me achieve what my supervisor wants from me"

Paradigm A will get the job done, but that's part of the problem, it just gets the job done. It's very "today" oriented without thinking about the future. It doesn't give your team the opportunity to grow.

The Paradigm B Catch

Paradigm B, I know what you're thinking: *I plan to stay in my position, so there won't be anywhere for them to go but out of my unit.* That may be true, but people who desire to be in formal leadership positions will find a way with you or without you. In paradigm B, you are building trust, fostering a team effort and building the leadership team you would like to work with. In considering Paradigm A, you could say you are better to dance with the devil you know and resist the inevitable growth and change that comes with any organization. Leadership classes and formal leadership development is important. The most important part of good succession planning and mentoring is done by giving people the opportunity to experience their own leadership style with your guidance, then debriefing the experience over a cup of coffee.

The next step

So you say you have paradigm B but don't know what to do next. Develop awareness for the natural leaders in your group. Who is asking management questions? Which team member brings issues to you with a solution? Give those people opportunities to experience operations beyond the department level. Discuss the business side of your industry, the part that they may not otherwise have the opportunity to experience and understand.

Next time you go out of town, designate someone who knows the business of your unit as "in charge" with a silent partner from your management group who can provide a safety net.

Think this takes too much out of you? Think about the last vacation you cancelled because you didn't make the time to mentor a trusted leader who could help you move your work unit's goals closer to completion. Someone to stand in the gap when you needed a little R & R.

So, are you an "I" leader or a "we" leader?

Leadership is communicating people's value and worth so well that they are inspired to see it in themselves

– Stephen Covey

Application

Do you have someone who can stand in for you today?

Who have you overlooked?

Do you have someone who is ready to step up a notch?

_____

_____

_____

_____

_____

Make training a rubber stamp

I was sitting with my boss and an administrative intern one day discussing the reorganization of our company's orientation process. Our conversation kept coming back to two all familiar themes: content and time. We were trying to condense our classroom orientation to one day from two. Being a trainer I had lots of issues with sacrificing any content. Finally, the administrative intern blurted out his true feelings, he said "regulatory training is just a rubber stamp anyway...isn't it?"

No, I am not writing this from prison so you can tell I didn't come across the table and strangle him. I did explain to him, however, that there are two types of education departments, those that "rubber stamp" safety and regulatory training, and those that believe it makes a difference in your team's safety. I submit to you that if you are running the former, close your door and turn in your keys now because you're worthless to your organization. If you are the latter, good for you, but for your team members' sake, be sure your training is relevant to the environment and that you are tied in with the people who track and trend issues at your place of work.

The power of preparation

Keep your training fresh. Think proactively about the "potential" for accidents and focus on prevention. There is a phenomenon I see when the disaster does happen and people respond appropriately. It goes something like this: "*See, we didn't need all that info after all.*" I say instead, "*Weren't you prepared well?*"

Remember all of the preparation for Y2K? We say nothing happened, but is that because nothing was going to? Or were we just prepared? Staff will always need some remedial safety training. We instituted a back safety program that was well-received, and low and behold, back injury numbers went down. The minute we took it off the list of annual education, declaring victory as if we'd just invented the polio vaccine, back injuries started to climb. What areas should you train in? Any that are likely to cause your team members lost time, life, limb or gainful employment.

Just Enough

Don't overkill the training; give your staff enough information to be competent, but not so much that you open the door to your office to find a hoard of pitchfork- and torch-wielding staff. You can look at regulatory training as a rubber stamp, but you will be ineffective and your students will smell your lack of commitment. I view it as the best way to send your team members whole and unscathed back to their families at the end of a shift.

Application

Is your training tied to organizational goals?

Do you have the right information to create worthwhile training?

Are you measuring the effectiveness of your training?

_____

_____

_____

_____

_____

_____

Are you a Zombie King or a Drama Queen?

Picture this: You're out of the office enjoying lunch with a friend and your cell phone rings. On the other end a frantic voice launches into a Chicken Little speech. *There's been a massive flood in the office; our people and our work are in grave danger!!! There's so much water I could've sworn I saw an Ark go by!!! We don't need the fire department we need the coast guard!!!!"* You rush to the scene of the emergency, throw open the door, fully expecting to see water pour out like Niagara Falls, only to see one of your team members mopping up the last of a coffee spill. Over dramatic? Yes. Helpful? Absolutely, if you want to raise your heart rate to work-out speed without breaking a sweat. In our personal and professional lives we have Drama Queens and we have Zombie Kings. You're acquainted with the Drama Queen; a Zombie King is her opposite. An extreme Zombie King doesn't move or show emotion regardless of the situation. In fact, he often doesn't give enough information about or credibility to a threat. Drama Queen or Zombie King? What we're looking for is a happy medium. Here's how you can tell the difference.

Drama Queen - to the extreme

- Any alteration to their world is cause for worry.

- Even the smallest incident is blown out of proportion with such vigor that everyone around initially plays into the drama.

- Eventually, People roll their eyes every time Drama Queen starts to speak.

- Warnings are unbelievable unless the evidence is validated by a third party.

If you hear "yeah....right...." when you open your mouth to speak you might want to check the other symptoms above.

Zombie King - to the extreme

- A severed arm is just a scratch.

- There's no problem if the air-conditioner breaks down at two o'clock in the afternoon; after all, it'll be cooler in the morning.

- The flood in the basement that took out half your business computer system will eventually dry once we stop the water "anybody got some gum?"

- Becomes unbelievable unless the evidence is validated by a third party

If people immediately get big eyes and run to find out what REALLY happened and how severe it is then you may want to explore the lists above. While both Drama Queens and Zombie Kings play important roles in keeping the communication bubbling, there are some ways to get yourself and others to the center of an issue.

If you identified yourself or someone around you as one of the above you can use a tip from the US Navy, a process called

SBAR which they use as framework for communication. Its stands for:

Situation: A brief description, emphasis on brief. Give it in 5 - 10 seconds. WHAT HAPPENED?

Back Ground: The context, objective data, the numbers. How did we get here? WHAT IS THE HISTORY?

Assessment: What is the problem? WHAT DO I THINK IS WRONG?

Recommendation: What do we need to do and when. WHAT DO I THINK NEEDS TO BE DONE?

You can use SBAR to move yourself toward the middle. Be self aware of which personality type you lean toward and use the framework to guide your conversations. If you are trying to manage a Zombie King or Drama Queen you can use the SBAR framework to filter the information by asking questions. It's a nice easy way to keep people focused in their communication so that they tell you where the fire is without going into the detail of where they got the matches.

Application

Take the assessment to decide which category you fall into.

Set an action plan to move your behavior more toward the center.

Use SBAR both to communicate and to get to the bottom of subjects.

_____

_____

_____

_____

_____

Celebrate your personal and professional journey

Several times a year I like to think back and reflect on past accomplishments and failures. We need to pat ourselves on the back for those things that we've done right, and think about the ingredients that made our projects and teams successful. We also need to do the same thing with projects and teams that haven't gone so well in an effort to minimize our mistakes in the future.

Try using these steps:

- Schedule time for review.

- Look over your calendar, all the way back over the preceding 12 months.

- Examine the reports and projects you've worked on.

- Catalogue what went right and what went wrong.

- Ask the "why" question that we ask everyone else so well.

- Think about what new skills and attitudes you may want to acquire in the next 12 months and yes, those you may want to lose.

- Identify resources that will help you achieve your goals.

One last thought, as organizations grow and change we often move to new and different programs to continue that growth. When you are transitioning to a new program, don't forget to thank the people who worked on the old program that grew your organization to its current level of effectiveness. You have to learn to walk before you can run, but I doubt anyone remembers the hand-holding before the first step. I don't remember saying, "*Thanks Mom, for teaching me how to walk.*" Celebrating success and transition validates the journey and keeps your effective people engaged.

Application

Find a quiet place to review the year.

Use the steps in this article to assess your progress.

Give yourself a written plan of application for improvement: the Start Doing, and the Stop Doing list.

_____

_____

_____

_____

_____

Creation v Implementation

It's time to present the outcome of your team's project to the senior leaders of your organization. The PowerPoint slides are a thing of beauty; the packets are neatly arranged at each seat. Almost immediately after beginning your presentation you notice that the CEO has a look on her face that makes you think she just bit into a big juicy lemon. Your outcome is not at all what she had in mind.

When we take on a project we must be keen to our team leaders' desires. One of my pre-facilitation questions is "are we talking about identification of direction or has that been defined?" If the leader who invited you to facilitate has an idea of where they want to end up in terms of outcome (like meeting a prescribed regulatory requirement or implementing a directive from the executive suite), your facilitation should focus on creative implementation methods that will support the desired outcome with the least amount of work. If the leader is seeking direction on the right path to take as in a strategy planning session or forward thinking initiative you have a little more latitude. You can focus on creatively identifying the desired outcome and then the implementation process.

Knowing where to focus your facilitation skills—implementation vs. creation—can save you and your team lots of heartache, grief and wasted time. Every facilitated event should start with a private discussion with the commissioning team leader so that you can achieve the desired outcome.

Application:

- Before you begin a project be sure you have clear expectations.

- Communicate those expectations to your project team members.

- Review the scope and guidelines of the project at the beginning of each meeting in order to stay on task.

_____

_____

_____

_____

_____

Valuing Differences Leveraging Strengths

I remember walking out of a meeting with a couple of colleagues who shared the same project. We had heard the same message and received the same direction from our senior management, but we each had a different take on the situation. Colleague One said, "*We need a celebration!*" Colleague Two said, "*We have to get some measurements and drill down.*" And Colleague Three said, "*We have to figure out our supporting processes.*"

You might think that the three different perceptions would spell disaster for the project. They're not on the same page, right? Actually, what looked like competing priorities is really complementing strengths. The "drill down artist" will figure things out and give the team direction; the "let's figure out how it works" person will figure out how to take the data and put it into tangible steps to make things better; and the "let's have a celebration" person will provide motivation and excitement around the project. They will also take the successes of the team, create the best party you've ever seen and make people feel good about their accomplishments.

Organizations need all three people. In fact, organizations need a multitude of people with complementing strengths to make things happen. We get into trouble when we take differing opinions and thoughts as personal attacks. When we work on a project we should leverage the strengths that people bring to the table.

Another item to consider in our busy lives is who else in the organization will be impacted by my decisions, my actions and the implementation of my team's plan. I'm not advocating analysis paralysis, however, many a good strategic plan has rested quietly on the shelf because it was not communicated or the right people weren't involved in the decision making.

The "watch out" in this scenario is just like our friends in the start of this article. People gravitate to what they like to do best, and Maslow remarked that the person that's good with a hammer thinks every solution is a nail. Don't get stuck on what YOU like to do best and appreciate. Look beyond your agenda. Developing a team means celebrating everyone's' contribution. A starting quarterback never did anything without the protection of the frontline.

Application

Do you know who you need on the team?

Whose special skills are not being used to their fullest potential?

Whose skills do you need to compensate for your weaknesses?

_____

_____

_____

_____

_____

Communicating policy and procedure

What I hear, I forget.
What I see, I remember.
What I do, I know - Lao Tzu

Healthcare is one of the most regulated industries in the world, but many of you face what you might consider overregulation as well. I don't know about you, but I'm surprised that those who regulate us haven't come up with a standard on how to drink water. I know what you're thinking; they probably have, and if they haven't, they are working on it.

It seems that every day we come up with a new or proposed change and if we don't, a regulatory agency does. So how do we help our staff navigate the sea of policies and procedures without running onto the rocks of noncompliance? I must confess that I don't always do as well as I should with this facet of management accountability.

The secret can be found in the quote at the start of this productivity tip, "what I do, I know." We frequently use passive methods of communication to distribute our policies and procedures. We talk about them in a staff meeting or we ask staff to "read and sign" a record that they have received and understand the policy put before them. For most policies and procedures this method is appropriate and fine. When polices involve employee and customer safety the importance of communication and retention move up the continuum a bit. Here are a few ideas to make your next policy and procedure change stick.

Policies and procedures that require a physical response

- Have staff read the policy out loud

- If the policy requires physical action, have staff perform a return demonstration

- Periodically quiz staff or ask them to "show and tell" how they would perform a particular task.

- To take the dread out of this method start with "If I were a surveyor with ABC regulatory agency and I asked you to demonstrate (insert procedure name here) what would you do?"

Policies and procedures that require a verbal response

- During your rounds, ask staff questions regarding important policies and procedures in a coaching manner (see phrasing above)

- Use phrasing that you think a regulatory surveyor might use

- Change up the way you ask the question so that staff are prepared to respond to different types of questioning.

What if they don't know the answer?

DO NOT

- Roll your eyes

- Sigh

- Look like you just ate a cockroach

DO

- Explain the policy and/or procedure

- Give the "why' not just the "what"

- Share additional resources

- Check back with the staff member to be sure the lesson stuck with them.

In the busy day-to-day of our work lives it's tough to get all of our staff to sit still for policy and procedure review. If we are available to our staff, accountable to the organization and validating retention, we can stay ready for CMS, TJC, OSHA, CDC, GAO, CAP, ACGME, HRSA, FDA, NFPA, EPA, NMRC, NMMRA and all of the other regulatory agencies that have the best of intentions, to keep our employees and our customers safe.

Make someone's day!!!

Application

The next time you have a policy or procedure to implement consider the physical or verbal response.

Once you've communicated the policy or procedure think of creative ways to reinforce it.

Is there someone on your team that would do a better job than you of communicating this policy or procedure?

_____

_____

_____

_____

_____

Meeting Attendance

"I hosted a party and no one came"

One of the challenges for any project manager is the "no show" participant. The meeting notice was sent to everyone's calendar, you were clear about the time, the place and what information to bring. You get to the meeting and your key team member doesn't show, causing wasted time and a delayed project. What drives these high maintenance participants to be "no shows" and how do we get them engaged? First, consider the reason for their behavior.

Competing priorities - is your initiative important enough to the organization to enjoy a high priority in the executive suites? It may be necessary for you to do a gut check with the powers that be. Revisit why the team was commissioned.

Unproductive meetings - If you have never-ending meetings with little to no progress, team member attendance usually starts to wane. People like their time to be respected and their contributions worthwhile. Make sure you are making and reporting progress. Thank people for their contributions.

Fear of the outcome - this is one of those "let's just not talk about it" facets of project management that usually comes into play behind the scenes. The department leader is scared that the outcome may include that nasty "change" word or worse yet, more work. I do agree that most process improvement initiatives should reduce work, emphasis on "most." In reality, to achieve meeting a stakeholder's need we sometimes create processes that in turn may create more work for our team members. I don't know of many managers who like to tell the team that the outcome includes more work. If the project does, set a meeting with this team member outside of the group to explore and address the issues. Make sure they feel supported and heard.

Assignments not completed - Rather than show up and report that they didn't do their home work, some team members will elect to just not show. It's really a face-saving move to buy them more time to complete their work. If you have a "no show" due to incomplete work you may want to check in with them mid-way between meetings to see if they need any help on their assignments. As leaders, it's our job to help people and teams be successful.

Wrong fit - The person chosen for the team may not be the right person for the job. If you can, find out whom the right person for the job is. Be sure that they are equipped and feel successful in each meeting.

Pre Meeting Strategies that can drive up your attendance.

- Have a clear goal and agenda for each meeting; don't just meet to meet.

- Meet with team members to discuss progress before the meeting occurs to be sure they have completed their assignment.

- Invite a Senior Leader to observe a meeting and be sure to highlight his or her attendance to all participants.

- Check the priority of the project against organizational goals.

- If you have a "no show," contact this person as soon as possible to find out the reason.

- Last but not least and only if you absolutely have to, discuss the situation with a more senior person in a constructive manner.

I close in reiterating the fact that we must consider the "reason" the person is a high maintenance team member first before we jump to strategies. Just as with process improvement, before you can apply the right strategy you must understand the root cause.

Postponement - the sincerest form of rejection.

Application

What is your agenda for your next meeting?

Do you know what you want to accomplish?

Have you checked with those who have assignments to be sure they are ready?

_____

_____

_____

_____

_____

Authenticity

1. The quality of being authentic or of established authority for truth and correctness.

2. Genuineness; the quality of being genuine or not corrupted from the original.

Authenticity from a leadership perspective is established moral authority. Not power from position, power from relationship. An authentic leader demonstrates authenticity through fairness in decision-making and dealings with staff, peers and superiors. Authentic leadership comes from within. It is character driven. To be an authentic leader you must know how you make decisions and how those decisions impact those around you. The quality of being authentic and not corrupted from the original requires regular introspection and course correction. Leaders today face the problem of popular opinion and likeability over substance and facts. Too often tough decisions are delayed or ignored out of fear of losing popularity.

Have you ever had this conversation, "What type of a mood is Bill in today? I want to ask for some time off." Do people know who you are? If your crew checks your attitude before they make a special request or approach you with a difficult issue, then you are probably lacking authenticity. Some people think that true leaders command fear and respect when they walk into a room, I believe that truly authentic leaders instantly make everyone comfortable when they walk into a room.

The Assessment

- Do people on your team wait to be told what to do?

- Do you have a designated ambassador to bring requests from the group to you?

- Is there healthy dialogue and alternative opinions expressed during your meetings?

- Have you held back on a decision out of fear of being un-popular?

- Have you implemented a decision you knew wasn't the best but would make you popular?

The Path

- Be introspective, dig deep into the motives that drive you.

- Identify and define your core values. Our core values drive our decision making. If we are uncomfortable with our decisions it's usually because we are in conflict with our values whether we have acknowledged them or not.

- Examine the decisions of the last week. Are they in concert or conflict with your core values? Actively work to be sure you are in concert with your core values in the future.

- Be yourself. Don't seek a cookie cutter method of leadership; it won't work. You have to let your leadership style morph to the situations you are handed. There is no one size fits all.

Authentic leaders exhibit integrity, honesty and fairness in their daily affairs. They make mistakes but apologize, give credit where credit is due and understand the power of trust and relationships. They believe in the importance of the individual. They consider the impact of their words and actions, but they don't shy away from tough decisions and know how to communicate change. Are you a trustworthy authentic leader? If your answer is "I don't know" you can take steps today to move in the right direction.

"The values you live by create the world you live in".

- Blaine Lee

Remember, beginning with this question will get you started, as you go through your authentic journey the answer to the question may change.

Application

Use the assessment to determine your authenticity

Resolve to take some introspective time to consider how you can improve

Use a trusted friend to provide insight into your leadership effectiveness.

_____

_____

_____

_____

_____

The Pattern of Cause and Effect

When I was a kid (chronologically) every time I passed my older brother in the hall he'd sock me in the arm. As a result, every time I walked past him in the hall I'd flinch, he'd hit, we'd move on and the natural law of older younger brothers was fulfilled. I remember the day I thought he grew a conscience. I was walking by him and in anticipation of the ritual beating my shoulder was about to take I flinched, not just a little flinch, I mean one of those body contorting, there's no way I'm getting out of this, here it comes flinches. My brother looked astonished and surprised. With a puzzled look on his face he said "why did you do that?" I don't know what caused his amnesia but I didn't question it. My brother never hit me again, but it took me at least seven more trips down that hallway without a shoulder pummeling before I stopped flinching. When I relayed this story to my mom as we were reminiscing one day she started to laugh and told me her older brother used to do that to her too.

Through the ages many authors, thinkers and business practitioners have given us great examples of how things should be done. They have told us and demonstrated what contributes to great relationships and great organizations. Attracting the right people, setting up the right systems, delivering on customer needs, have all been thought through yet we still don't capitalize on the sage wisdom of the past and present.

We choose to repeat mistakes instead of adopting and adapting proven cause and effect patterns in both our personal and professional lives.

The patterns we set up can be hard to change. My brother stopped hitting but I kept flinching because of the cause and effect pattern we'd set up in the relationship. As we work on our personal and professional cause and effect patterns we need to keep in mind that when we change, we must communicate through our words and actions. The most important thing a leader can do when making a positive change from a negative pattern of cause and effect is to be overt about it. I mean BROADCAST, BROADCAST, BROADCAST. If you miss this step your staff will continue to flinch, they will look for all of the reasons you haven't changed instead of all of the reasons you have.

Application

Examine your cause and effect patterns

Identify behaviors and patterns that may be destructive

Resolve to bring constructive positive contributions

Stay the course; it may take time for people to get used to the new you.

_____

_____

_____

_____

_____

A final word

This helpful little book would not be complete without acknowledgement of my reliance and faith in Jesus Christ as my Lord, Savior and director of my path.

Psalm 121:1-2 I lift up my eyes to the hills, where does my help come from, my help comes from the Lord, the Maker of heaven and earth